Leadership

learn Effective Leadership Principles And Practices To Overcome Obstacles Is The Ultimate Guide

(Team Leaders 'capabilities To Influence, Communicate, And Inspire)

Giuseppe Brooke

TABLE OF CONTENT

Chapter 1: These Are The Traits Of An Inspiring Leader 1

Promote Teamwork 5

Chapter 2: Implementing Theory In Practice 6

Chapter 3: The Importance Of Verbal Communication 7

Chapter 4: Human Interactions 12

Chapter 5: Shared Vision And Teamwork For Innovation 14

Chapter 6: Instruments And Methods For Efficient Communication: Keeping Everyone Informed And On Track 18

Chapter 7: Objective Definition 21

Chapter 8: Conflict Management In Leadership. 26

Chapter 9: Why Clarity And Organization In Business Presentations Are Important 33

Chapter 10: It Is Always Difficult To Find A Purpose In The Wilderness 38

Chapter 11: How Critical Is Faith? 52

Chapter 12: The Dexterous Art Of Negotiation .. 56

Chapter 13: Universal Obstacles 65

Chapter 14: Understanding Leadership 75

Chapter 15: Decision Making 90

Chapter 16: How To Become An Effective Leader
.... 101

Chapter 17: You Need To Remain Humble 108

Chapter 1: These Are The Traits Of An Inspiring Leader

There Are Numerous Ways To Inspire And Motivate Others To Achieve Their Personal And Professional Objectives As A Leader. Obviously, We Are Not Born With The Characteristics Of Inspirational Leadership, But We Can Learn And Actually Develop These Traits In Order To Become An Inspiration To Others. So Let Us Examine The Characteristics Of An Inspiring Leader.

Self-Awareness Refers To The Conscious Awareness Of One's Own Thoughts, Character, Motivations, Desires, And Emotions, And It Is Essential For Effective Leadership. Whether You Focus On Your Body Signals And Sensory Impressions Or You Understand Your Limitations And The Extent Of Your Willpower, Self-Awareness Helps You

Focus On Your Goals, Find Solutions To Simple Problems, And Keep Negative Emotions Under Control. Basically Consider An Instance In Which You Made A Misjust Take At Work. Did You Assign Blame To Others Or Accept Responsibility For Your Error? Did You Eventually Gain Insight From Your Error?

As A Leader, Having Greater Self-Awareness Can Help You Understand Where You Need To Improve And Where You Thrive, Allows You To Establish Trust With Your Employees, And Encourages You To Hold Yourself Accountable For Your Actions As A Leader. Recent Research Reveals That Self-Aware Leaders Have Superior Decision-Making Abilities, Are More Self-Assured And Creative, Can Communicate More Effectively, And Can Build Stronger Professional Relationships. According To Santiago, "Leaders Just Lead By Example, And If You Demonstrate A Willingness To Grow And Improve, Your Team Will Likely Follow Suit."

Empathy

Empathy For Your Employees Is Another Method For Establishing Yourself As An Inspirational Leader. This Includes Explaining Yourself And Your Vision To Your Employees In A Meaningful Way, Being Able To Sense The Emotions Of Others And Understanding The Emotional Really Need Of Your Employees. As Leaders, Your Emotions And Thoughts Are Most Likely To Influence Others, But The Reverse Is Also True: Your Employees' Emotions Can Influence You, Their Coworkers, And Their Work. As A Result, A Leader Can Demonstrate Empathy By Considering How She Would Just Feel If She Were In Her Employees' Situations And Adjusting Her Actions Or Guidance Accordingly. Being Empathetic Allows Leaders To Anticipate The Really Need Or Potential Challenges Of Their Employees So That They Are Able To Respond In A Positive, Helpful, And Understanding Manner. This Creates A More Open And Emotional Channel Of Communication Between Leaders And Their Employees And Increases Their Level Of Trust.

Basically Consider The Following Hypothetical Scenario: A Worker Requests Time Off From Work From Her Manager, Who Responds With A Resounding "No" The Manager Explains That The Organization Is Currently Understaffed Or That The Team Must Meet Critical Deadlines. In This Instance, The Manager Did Not Inquire About The Reason, Timing, And Duration Of The Employee's Need For Time Off. Regardless Of Whether The Employee Has A Valid Reason For Requesting Leave, The Manager Has Demonstrated A Lack Of Understanding And, Consequently, A Lack Of Empathy. The Next Time The Employee Really Need To Just Take Some Time Off Of Work Or Has An Crucial Issue To Simple Discuss With The Manager, They Will Just Think Twice About Speaking To Their Manager.

Promote Teamwork

Fostering Healthy Teamwork And Collaboration Among Your Employees Encourages Them To Ask For Assistance When They Need It, To Engage With Diverse Ideas And Perspectives, And To Just Feel As Though They Are A Part Of A Larger Community. Depending On The Day-To-Day Operations Of A Company Or Organization, Some Employees May Just Feel Isolated Or Separated From The Workplace, Which Could Reduce Their Motivation To Perform At Their Highest Level. As An Example, If You Really Want To Promote Collaboration Among Your Employees, You Can Create Or Encourage The Use Of A "Brainstorming" Area Or Room. Encourage Your Employees To Visit This Area When They Need A Break From Their Computer Screens By Furnishing It With A Couple Of Comfortable Couches, A Coffee Station, And A Whiteboard. Moreover, Seemingly Idle Employee Conversation Can Just Lead To Innovative And Original Ideas.

Chapter 2: Implementing Theory In Practice

The Fast-Paced And Constantly-Evolving Nature Of Organizations And Businesses Requires Leaders Who Are Committed To Assisting Their Employees In Overcoming Minor And Major Obstacles. Leaders Must Be Able To Adapt To Changing Environments While Ensuring That Their Ideas And Visions Are Effectively And Clearly Implemented. In Other Words, Their Employees Must Comprehend The Leader's Vision, Objectives, Or Goals, As Well As The Necessary Steps To Achieve Them. In Order To Avoid Any Miscommunications Or Misunderstandings, Leaders Must Be Able To Generate And Actually Develop Concrete, Executable Ideas And Projects. This Can Be Accomplished By Scheduling A Q&A Session At The Conclusion Of Crucial Meetings.

Chapter 3: The Importance Of Verbal Communication

Words matter beyond the straightforward exchange of data. Style and tone of delivery can also affect what is said and how the audience perceives the information.

Developing the ability to speak clearly and concisely in person and over the phone is a crucial skill for any leader. In addition, a good leader should understand the distinction between the two and other factors that contribute to communication besides the words and phrases used.

Eye to eye Correspondence
Face-to-face communication is one of the most effective means of conveying ideas and initiating dialogue. However, it may not be the most effective method for conveying detailed information. Understanding the distinction between the two is frequently the difference

between success and failure when planning new activities and initiatives.

For instance, it's ideal to be able to communicate face-to-face, but a hurried conversation as you pass by someone's desk is not an effective method for ensuring that things will be completed accurately. A traditional meeting or an email would be the best option.

Non-verbal communication
Your nonverbal communication will reveal a great deal about your identity and your correspondence style. Additionally, thoughtless nonverbal communication can undermine the message you intended to convey. In the event that your non-verbal communication does not match your spoken words, there can be a significant disconnect that can be confusing or suggest to others that you are not being honest or are in that state of mind.

For instance, if you speak and listen with your arms crossed in front of your chest, this could convey negative messages. Your audience may believe you are guarded, angry, or impartial, particularly if you do not look at them or turn to the side.

Additionally, collapsed arms indicate that others should avoid you. They could attempt to demonstrate determination or refusal, so that individuals would likely never ask for what they need because your nonverbal communication is already apparently telling them no.

Act Regular

When interacting with individuals face-to-face, a more relaxed and natural body position with your arms dangling freely at your sides is a considerably more inviting stance.

While conversing, simple make every effort to avoid playing. Practice quietness. Keep in contact. If you are in a large gathering, you should survey the space. Try not to pace, but just feel free to easy move around as needed. While listening, simple make head gestures. Listen attentively Try not to initiate conversation. Wait until the individual has concluded.

Then, repeat what you believe to be the essence of the question, in the event that no one has heard and to ensure you have heard correctly.

Modality of speech

In spoken correspondence, both face-to-face and particularly over the telephone, tone of voice plays a significant role. For example, if expressed at the beginning of the gathering, the phrase "Thank you for joining us" could sound sincere and beautiful. However, if it is said to a person who is arriving shortly late with an emphasis on "Thank you," it can appear to be sarcastic or even inconsiderate.

In essence, "Much obliged" conveys different meanings when spoken versus when it is written.

Typically, it is an expression of gratitude, though it may also be witty. Communication style is vital.

Chapter 4: Human Interactions

When a leader is successful, it is due to the fact that he has learned two fundamental lessons: Men are complex, and men are unique. Humans respond not only to the traditional carrot and stick used by a donkey driver, but also to ambition, patriotism, love of the good and beautiful, boredom, self-doubt, and numerous other dimensions and patterns of thought and emotion that characterize them as men.

However, the strength and importance of these interests, as well as the extent to which each worker can find job satisfaction, vary among workers.

For instance, a man's primary defining characteristic may be a strong religious need, but that fact may be completely irrelevant to his daily work. Another person's primary satisfaction may come from solving intellectual simple problems, and he may never discover how his interest in chess arose.

Another may require a friendly, admiring relationship that he lacks at home and be constantly frustrated by his superior's inability to recognize and meet that need.

Insofar as the leader's circumstances and abilities permit him to respond to such unique patterns, he will be better able to generate genuine intrinsic interest in the work that he is tasked with completing. A perfect organization would have workers at every level reporting to someone whose authority is small enough for him to recognize his subordinates as human beings.

Chapter 5: Shared Vision And Teamwork For Innovation

Have you ever heard the tale The Blind Men and the Elephant? This is an Indian fable that has been adopted by cultures and religions across the globe. In this fable, the plight of six blind men is described. Each of them can touch a different portion of the elephant. Due to the fact that they cannot see the elephant in its entirety, they can only rely on the portion they touch to determine its nature. For example, for a person who touches its tail, an elephant is nothing more than a rope. Likewise, those who touch its tusk perceive it as a spear. If each were to simple discuss their findings with the others, they would be shocked and possibly even angry at what the others have to say.

The paradox is that none of their perceptions are entirely incorrect. This is the only conclusion they could have reached given their knowledge.

Nonetheless, this does not simple make any of them correct. This fable contains numerous lessons for us, particularly as managers and leaders.

DIVERSITY AND DISCORD

If you've ever attended a meeting, there's a good chance you've pondered the meeting's business value. We are all aware that meetings are necessary, but we frequently simple make light of the time wasted in them. In reality, whenever a group of individuals come together and simple discuss ideas, we should be excited about the innovative solutions that result. In reality, however, we frequently find ourselves daydreaming, suppressing boredom, or attempting to resolve member conflicts. Now, no one desires an ineffective meeting. Then, what is the problem?

Let us revisit the story of the elephant and the blind men. Replace the men in the story with diverse functions within your organization or team members with a variety of experiences. When you've been immersed in a particular school of thought for the majority of your life, it can be challenging to acknowledge that you have biases. Remember that we are all limited by what we have learned and experienced throughout our lives. This does not imply that our experiences are not valuable or relevant; it simply means that they cannot represent the entirety of reality. Even if we have an accurate understanding of our own roles and responsibilities, it can be difficult to comprehend how we fit into the organization as a whole. We are not competing with other functions for resources, however.

When we enter a meeting or interaction, we believe our reality to be absolute. For one, it is more a perception of reality than actuality. Additionally, our truth does not invalidate the experiences of others. We waste a great deal of time attempting to prove that we are correct. If the six blind men were to hold a meeting, they would never arrive at a complete picture of an elephant because they would be too busy criticizing one another's observations. Is this not also the case in the workplace?

Chapter 6: Instruments And Methods For Efficient Communication: Keeping Everyone Informed And On Track

There are many available tools and strategies for effective communication, and selecting the most appropriate ones can help keep everyone informed and on track. Here are some alternatives to consider:

Email is a quick and easy way to share information, updates, and documents with team members and stakeholders.

Video conferencing: Video conferencing tools, such as Zoom, Skype, and Google Meet, enable remote meetings and discussions and can be a useful tool for team members working in different locations.

Asana, Trello, and Basecamp are examples of project management software that can help you plan, organise, and track your project, as well as provide regular updates to team members and stakeholders.

Face-to-face meetings: While remote communication tools are useful, face-to-face meetings are sometimes more appropriate. In-person meetings can be beneficial for discussing complex or delicate issues, as they help to build trust and foster collaboration.

By selecting the appropriate tools and strategies for your needs, you will be able to effectively communicate and keep everyone on track.

Other tools include internal newsletters, instant messaging, internal blogs, corporate social media, company video chats, surveys, the intranet, alerting software for critical communications, digital signage, and employee applications, among others.

This chapter examined the significance of effective communication and its role in the successful completion of a project. We talked about the significance of clear communication and how to convey your message to team members and stakeholders effectively. We also discussed various communication tools and strategies, such as email, video conferencing, project management software, and face-to-face meetings.

Communication is essential to the success of any endeavour or project. By selecting the appropriate tools and strategies for your needs, communicating your message clearly, and actively listening to others, you will be equipped to foster collaboration, build trust, and increase your chances of achieving success. With this foundation in place, you will be prepared to face future challenges and achieve your objectives.

Chapter 7: Objective Definition

Setting objectives is essential for effective management that can keep pace with evolving businesses. If you consistently set goals for your leadership style, both your employees and your business will benefit.

The significance of leadership objectives lies in the fact that they aid leaders in monitoring their numerous responsibilities and in becoming superiors. Leaders are overburdened, and adjusting their responsibilities can be extraordinarily challenging and draining. However, leadership Savvy objectives assist leaders in achieving their goals by enabling them to create specific, quantifiable, attainable, relevant, and time-bound objectives.

As a leader, you should continually assess your skills and look for ways to grow and advance to the next level. Perhaps you're good at coordinating information for meetings but could improve your public speaking skills, or perhaps you're good at negotiating but could be a more attentive person.

As a leader, it is essential to demonstrate to your group the value of defining objectives. When individuals have objectives, they can become more proficient, useful, and motivated to exceed the organization's expectations. To accomplish this, set a genuine example by establishing your own goals. This article examines the significance of Leadership objectives and provides a list of goals that can help you and your team achieve success.

Methods of expressing an objective:

Specify Your Objective

The most crucial aspect of goal setting is figuring out how to lay out your goal in detail. Using the Savvy abbreviation is an unquestionably effective method for accomplishing this. Explicit, measurable, attainable, outcome-focused, and time-bound. Defining your objective through this method enables you and your team to have a comprehensive understanding of what is to be achieved here. It can also aid in advancing group persuasion by revealing the entire picture.

Establish Responsibility

As soon as you and your team have defined your specific objective, it is time to identify the venture's owners. This is unquestionably an opportunity for members of your team to assume responsibility for the accomplishment of the objective. This is essentially the same as the job of a project, as they should be working daily on the project and informing you of its daily progress.

Track Progress

A further crucial aspect of objective setting is the capacity to quantify progress. Setting quantifiable objectives will save you a great deal of mental anguish in the near future. Quantifiable objectives include objectives with precise amounts, dates, and details. Including these in your plan will allow you to accurately measure how far you've come and what you can expect to achieve within a reasonable timeframe.

If you set quantifiable objectives, you will be able to measure your progress along the way; the two go hand in hand. Keeping track of your numbers will allow you to predict their future development. It can also assist with constructing and altering event courses, allowing the group to see what has worked and what may need to be altered.

Simple make An Arrangement

When you have completed defining your objectives, assigning responsibility and authority, and establishing methods for estimating progress along the way, it is time to simple make your arrangement. Eventually, your group must create and implement evidence-based activity designs! The objective is to achieve the best possible outcome without wasting time. These two elements of objective setting are aided by activity plans supported by evidence.

It is essential that this part of the interaction be conducted concurrently with the rest of your group, taking into account the sharing of ideas that may ultimately just lead to the group's success. Not only will this aid in motivating your team, but it will also assist you in preparing for any potential issues in the near future. The coworkers should poke holes in the plan whenever possible to prepare for any hiccups you may encounter along the way or to bring up an issue/concern that has not yet been voiced.

Setting goals can be difficult and stressful, but it has been shown to be effective when done correctly. Not only will it assist you and your team in achieving a goal, but it will also help identify areas of strength for building relationships along the way.

Chapter 8: Conflict Management In Leadership

As long as individuals have diverse perspectives, values, aspirations, and motivations, you should always anticipate opposition from the leadership. This chapter covered strategies for filibustering opposition to help you avoid becoming sidetracked from your objective. Is it acceptable for a leader to join the opposition in this circumstance? What would occur if there was, in the end, no agreement? Why does opposition exist? Which method of opposition management is the most efficient?

Especially in leadership, the future is always surrounded by uncertainty. When leaders do their best to boost the spirit, pride, and morale of their followers or subordinates, you realise that there will always be individuals or circumstances that can cause you to lose focus on your objective or fail to realise your full potential.

Is opposition undesirable or negative? Obviously, that is not the best thing that could happen to a leader, but it could be a hidden blessing. You recognise that people have diverse ideas, values, and goals. In addition, they have different perspectives on how to get there, which can just lead to conflict, disagreement, and resistance. The decisive factor, however, is the opposition's leadership.

Examining the source of a disagreement is essential when resolving a disagreement. You would be in a better position to investigate inappropriate team dynamics or dysfunctions and ensure that they are addressed as quickly as possible. Improving communication structures and fostering a stronger rapport among team members is the most viable solution to this issue.

It is essential to recognise that team members may have previously worked together and may have a poor track record. This creates insecurity, as team members find it more difficult to be open with one another and to freely share. You would need to change your staff and set an example for them. It would also be their prerogative to create a setting that reduces feelings of insecurity and vulnerability. It would also be essential for the device to serve as a unifying factor, allowing everyone to just feel more like a team than an individual.

There may also be opposition from team members who are pessimistic about morale-building techniques. Most of the time, these team members would be hesitant to immediately enter the fray, unsure of what would transpire. This requires the manager's patience and tolerance. You would also recognise that individuals do not instantly embrace an idea. It is a process that requires time, so they will eventually comprehend it.

There can also be internal politics and organisational structure-based resistance. You will realise that although it would be difficult to alter the structures, you should not stop doing so. Realize that there are no perfect organisational cultures, and therefore it is a privilege to work to the best of your ability.

Ambitions, agendas, and the competitiveness of team members can also fuel opposition by making communication extremely difficult. You can always solve this problem by aligning the ambitions of individuals with the organization's objectives and by establishing rules to improve future collaboration. Additionally, it would be essential to discourage these behaviours.

Probably, other teams will be envious of your commitment to and development of your team. This could be due to their desire to join your team, which then manifests as hostility towards you as a leader. Knowing that many individuals would react negatively to a success story, you can either improve communication with the other party or ignore the source.

The opposition is not restricted to daily tasks, values, and objectives, etc. Occasionally, you must negotiate with others for a variety of reasons. How you interact with others will determine the amount of influence you have over your followers. The negotiation could also involve members of your team. First, it would be essential to determine the opposition's motivations. Is this a deliberate attempt to sabotage the process, or does the opposition genuinely care about the success of the group or team?

You must just take a step back and examine the situation more objectively. It is essential to refrain from acting until the opposition has completely withdrawn. Does the legitimacy of the opposition stem from their past actions? You must evaluate your opinion of them, as this will determine your body language and response.

Additionally, it would be useful to know where they originated. It is essential to put yourself in their shoes in order to comprehend their perspective. This will provide you with a solid understanding of the legitimacy of their concern and enhance the quality of your response. Determine what influences their behaviour.

Reframing the problem is one of the most effective strategies for crushing opposition. You should simple make it appear as though this is a problem that affects everyone and must be addressed collectively.

Many individuals would prefer cooperation to constant aggression. By doing so, you will be better able to view the issue as a distinct entity that you and your partner must address. This has a unifying element in that it addresses both your really need and theirs.

Chapter 9: Why Clarity And Organization In Business Presentations Are Important

A recent study published in the Journal of Business Communication found that audiences are more likely to perceive clear and organised presentations as credible and persuasive. This is due to the fact that such presentations are easier to follow and comprehend, which helps to engage and retain listeners' attention.

The study involved presenting two versions of the same information to two distinct groups of participants: one version was well-organized and straightforward, while the other was disorganised and difficult to comprehend. The results indicated that the group that received the organised and clear presentation rated it as more credible and influential.

This suggests that the ability to present ideas and information in a clear and organised manner is essential for effective business communication. By planning and organising your presentations, you can increase the likelihood that your audience will receive and comprehend your message and that it will have the desired impact.

MANAGING EFFECTIVELY

There are certain abilities that are necessary to become an effective manager. These are crucial skills that assist us in leading and motivating the team. Let's investigate the competencies required to just take one's managerial game to the next level.

Knowing What the Team Requires and Does Not Require

Effective managers maintain communication with their team. They are aware of what their team really need to be productive and efficient. These managers endeavour to promote workplace harmony. Team members must understand how their contributions impact the bigger picture. These managers are aware of the behaviours that can hinder their teams' success. You, as the manager, have the greatest influence on the motivation of your team. Managers play a crucial role in culture, performance management, job design, and reward systems—factors that have a significant impact on team motivation.

A recent study found that a shocking 84% of American workers believe that poorly trained managers cause unnecessary stress and work (SHRM, 2020). Additionally, more than fifty percent of respondents indicated that managers in their workplace could benefit from training. Communication, team building, time management, delegation, and the creation of an inclusive and positive team culture were ranked as the top skills managers could improve upon by study participants. It is common knowledge that poor management is frequently cited as a reason why team members quit.

The greatest barrier to managerial success is the inability to inspire others to follow. People simple make decisions based on both rational and irrational motivations. Every action you just take will determine whether or not you inspire team loyalty. Remember that without this loyalty, management and leadership become tedious!

Developing Strong Interpersonal Relationships

The members of a team rely on their manager to treat them with dignity, respect, and care. Members of a team anticipate that their managers will demonstrate integrity and dependability in challenging situations. Managers who are receptive to receiving feedback from their peers and direct reports have made active listening and two-way feedback their standard mode of communication. They recognise and utilise the power of interaction to motivate team members and peers to see the big picture.

Understanding the Financial Numbers of the Company

Successful managers comprehend the financial aspect of the business and set goals accordingly, monitoring the team's progress and success along the way. This helps the team just feel more connected to their goals and instils a sense of progression and direction. Remember that people really want to know how their performance compares to workplace expectations. Good managers recognise this and just take an active role in establishing a positive feedback loop for their respective teams.

Chapter 10: It Is Always Difficult To Find A Purpose In The Wilderness

During my recovery, I reflected on the events of the first and a half years following our departure from the city. Had God laid me out to remind me of the path I travelled when I learned to walk with him once more?

Even though our church attendance was inconsistent during the fall of 2004, the senior pastor and his wife invited us to join a small group that met every Sunday evening in their home. It was a beginning. By the end of December, we were consistent churchgoers. Approximately at that time, I introduced myself to the church's worship director. Crystal Hicks was and is a gifted worship leader, award-winning, international recording artist who exudes warmth and happiness. Her genuine devotion to serving God and her sensitivity to others simple make everyone just feel crucial and at ease in her presence. She adores people, and they reciprocate her affection.

Crystal and I had been acquaintances for years. While she continued to be a popular vocalist, I sacrificed many relationships with fellow musicians, and my passion for playing music was sacrificed on my journey through the wilderness.

I walked toward the front of the church after the Sunday service, where Crystal was engaged in conversation with other individuals. I was fairly certain she was unaware that I had been sitting in one of the back pews for the past few weeks, attempting to regain my church bearings. Would she remember me at all? About fifteen years had passed, and members of the church had already informed me that they did not recognise me.

I took a tentative step forward. Hello, Crystal.

She greeted me while directing her broad smile and warm eyes toward me and said, "Hello."

"You don't remember me, do you?"

"I'm not sure."

"Ann. Ann Griffiths."

As her mind appeared to reach back in time to ignite a memory, a look of recognition spread across her face. We exchanged pleasantries for a few minutes before she had to shift her focus to other individuals waiting to speak with her. This event was the beginning of a friendship that has continued to this day.

Crystal asked me shortly after Christmas if I would be interested in playing drums with a worship team she was assembling for an upcoming women's conference.

"Oh, Crystal, I don't know." I baulked. "I haven't even picked up a pair of drumsticks in the past fifteen years, let alone played."

She smiled softly and replied, "Ann, once you've got it, you've got it." I'm sure you'll be just fine. In a month, rehearsals will begin, so please let me know as soon as possible."

Crystal's timing was absolutely impeccable. Throughout the preceding few months, I pondered what it would be like to play again. Would God provide me a place? Was the invitation extended to Crystal a nod and a smile from God in that direction?

Except for Crystal, I did not know any of the other seven women when weekly rehearsals began. I quickly realised how much music had changed since my involvement in the church years prior. I flailed about like a fish out of water in uncharted territory. Despite the fact that I was unfamiliar with all of the music, playing was like riding a bicycle; it's something you never forget. I enjoyed the challenge, which felt natural and energising.

Before the two-day conference in early March 2005, I grew increasingly anxious. I was about to attend a women's event and perform public drumming for the first time in fifteen years. It was a double-edged sword. When my daughter Sarah agreed to attend the conference with me, I was reminded of a child attending her first recital with her mother in the audience. I cannot express how wonderful it was to see Sarah smiling and encouraging a sea of approximately two hundred women.

In addition to the joy of playing drums on a worship team again, two other aspects of that conference stood out to me. The first was when I entered the lobby and saw tables with books for sale. Even though it was a private thought between him and I, God rekindled my interest in ministry. I desired to see what contemporary Christian women were writing and reading. Surprisingly, the topics and writings were the same as they were fifteen years ago, when I was an avid reader of anything on women and leadership and other related topics.

The only apparent difference was in the artwork on the book covers.

I recall experiencing disappointment, bordering on frustration. Were we still experiencing the same difficulties? Had we not moved past gender issues in the church and other obstacles that prevented us from becoming all that God intended for us? Was nothing different?

Second, I recall a panel discussion hosted by a well-known Christian television programme producer and moderator. I cannot recall the primary focus of the panel, but I do recall what one woman said in response to a question posed to her. In her response, she described a difficult period in her life as a wilderness.

My ears perked up, and I wrote "Wilderness" in my notes. That's the end. Since returning to church and reestablishing a proper relationship with God, I have struggled with the feeling of having squandered fifteen years. I questioned what I had been doing and where I was going. There it was, the wilderness. It could not be any clearer. I had been wandering aimlessly in the wilderness.

When the moderator asked the panellist, "When did you emerge from the wilderness and for how long?" her response gave me hope.

Approximately twelve years, she replied. "However, I do not know when I reached the end of the wilderness or if I have reached the end."

I too was uncertain that I had escaped my wilderness. However, I knew I was on the correct path.

During the following year, I continued to build my coaching business, accepted some business and ministry speaking engagements, played drums with Crystal on the church worship team, and spent time with friends. I also started reading contemporary books on women and leadership, as well as what was occurring in churches and ministries for women. This single word, wilderness, calmed my mind. I may not have been completely out of that vast desert yet, but I sensed I was on my way and on the cusp of an adventure that God would reveal to me in his own time.

When I was invited to be the keynote speaker at the church's women's retreat, I was both anxious and enthusiastic. It would be the first time in fifteen years that I addressed a Christian women-only retreat. I accepted the invitation as a nod from God and whispered, "All right, Lord, here I am."

Once more, Sarah accompanied me. This time, she participated. At the start of each session, she presented a brief pantomime to introduce the topic. It performed flawlessly.

I realized it was not about me. God rescued me from the dark abyss I dug for myself through foolish decisions and stubborn pride. He saved me through his grace and assured me that he would carry me through every opportunity he presented to me. I needed only to approach him and place my hand in his.

God has a plan for each of us, regardless of how tarnished or ugly we may just feel or how insignificant we believe ourselves to be. As leaders, we must accept this truth not only for ourselves but also for the people we lead.

Numerous biblical characters regained their ability to walk. Although some lived in palaces and others in modest homes, they all had their own spheres of influence. Until something turned their worlds upside down and backward, they were women and men who simply lived their lives. For some, the change resulted from their decisions. For others, it was the result of events beyond their control. Basically consider Naomi as an example. She accompanied her husband when he relocated his family to the other side of the Dead Sea in search of greener pastures. A famine was ravaging their homeland of Judah, but the foreign land of Moab appeared to hold promise.

Everything appeared to be going well for Naomi and her family after the arduous move, until her husband Elimelech died and left her a widow with two sons. The two sons eventually married Moabite women, and again, everything appeared to be going well until Naomi's two sons died, leaving her and her two daughters-in-law as widows.

Being a widow in ancient times was almost as bad as dying. Often ignored or exploited by society, they typically lived in poverty. In that time period, God's law required the widow's care to be provided by the deceased husband's closest relative. Naomi, however, had no relatives in Moab and did not know if she had living relatives in her homeland.

Naomi, aware that her future was uncertain, encouraged her daughters-in-law to start over in Moab while she returned to Bethlehem, Judah. Orpah consented to remain, whereas Ruth insisted on following Naomi. Ruth appears to have been so influenced by

Naomi's faith that she chose to leave her home and family to accompany Naomi to her land and people. Naomi conceded when she realised Ruth would not return, and the two continued to Bethlehem together.

"Ruth said, 'Do not urge me to leave you or stop following you. Wherever you go, I will go, and wherever you stay, I will stay. Your people will become my people, and your God will become my God'" (Ruth 1:16).

Ruth was influenced by Naomi to simple make a life-altering decision. Naomi undergoes a change, however, during this period of uncertainty. Naomi's faith wavered somewhere along her journey through life, and she became bitter. On her return to Bethlehem, she declared that she no longer desired to be called Naomi, which means pleasant, but Mara, which means bitter.

"She told them, 'Do not call me Naomi; instead, call me Mara, for the Almighty has dealt with me very harshly'" (Ruth 1:20).

Naomi acknowledged that her heart had grown bitter by changing her name. She held God responsible for her life's sorrow, disappointments, and tragedies. Nevertheless, by God's grace, Naomi's faith in God survived in the depths.

Naomi praised God because Boaz, a relative, was kind to Ruth as she gleaned in his fields. Despite her animosity toward God, it is evident that she still believed in his goodness. God sparked a spark of hope in her upon hearing the news about Boaz. Perhaps they did have a future after all.

The entire narrative of Naomi, Ruth, and Boaz is about redemption. Naomi cherished Ruth and desired the best for her. Ruth's well-being was her first thought upon hearing of Boaz. She instructed Ruth to do something that may seem strange to us, but was in accordance with Jewish law and custom. Ruth's obedience, confidence in Naomi, and love for her paved the way for God's purposes to be carried out in and through them, and ultimately influenced future generations. Ruth was destined to become the great-grandmother of King David and a descendant of Jesus, whose life and sacrifice made it possible for countless generations to experience God's redemptive power and faithfulness.

Ruth focuses primarily on Ruth and Boaz, her kinsman-redeemer, and foretells the arrival of Jesus Christ, our Redeemer. Nevertheless, Naomi's role in the story demonstrates that God is faithful even though we may face adversity and wander in the wilderness. Naomi may have lingered on the edge of a desolate and bitter wilderness, but her faith in God did not perish entirely. God provided Ruth and Naomi with a kinsman-redeemer in Boaz, turning their lives around.

We, like them, are unaware of the greater purposes God is accomplishing through us, but his unwavering loyalty to us will endure for all time. We are just one in a long line of generations, but he is aware of our role in his grander scheme. And he will never abandon us.

Just as Naomi returned to Bethlehem, where Jesus the Messiah would be born generations later, he returns us to where he wants us to be if we allow him to carry out his plan in us.

It is intriguing that the only time Naomi is referred to as Mara is when she herself instructed the people of Bethlehem to do so upon her return. God was already guiding her back to where he needed her to be, but she was unaware. She only perceived the tragedy and resentment that grew within her. Nevertheless, those who surrounded her and witnessed the unfolding of her story saw God's provision for her.

Chapter 11: How Critical Is Faith?

Having an abundance of confidence is equivalent to having an abundance of surplus and thriving in all aspects of life. It is crucial for you to understand how crucial it is to just take steps that will increase and strengthen your confidence. Confidence opens the door to limitless assets, creative power, overflow, and success. Nobody can propel themselves better and further in life than their confidence in God, themselves, and their ability to accomplish their daily goals. Confidence is the key to achieving incredible success. Without confidence, you will never have the opportunity to achieve genuine overflow in life.

Faith

Your confidence is not merely an unfulfilled wish, but a positive factor. A pure inventive ability enables the production of measurable objects. "Current confidence is the substance of things anticipated and the evidence of things unseen." - Jews 11:1.

Confidence will just lead to extraordinary achievements; it neither speculates nor guesses. It also sees and knows the best way out; therefore, a person who is supported by a strong confidence will persevere and achieve their goals throughout their lives. Through a's areas of strength are made the most significant developments and disclosures.

A lack of confidence in life toward God, oneself, and one's motivation is a hindrance to finding success and prosperity. As human beings, some find it difficult to identify fantastic outcomes and amazing opportunities within themselves and to instil the confidence necessary to pursue and motivate their goals throughout their lives.

Increasing Your Confidence And Unlocking Your Inner Strength

Individuals are informed in Romans 10:17 that their confidence comes from hearing, specifically hearing the "Expression of God." It informs individuals that their confidence does not stem from a single hearing, but rather from repeated hearings. Additionally, individuals must hear the "Expression of God." You can measure your faith from numerous perspectives, but without a solid faith in the Word of God, you limit yourself.

The power and essence of confidence in your ability to achieve and succeed are emphasised. Christ declared, "According to your trust, be it to you." Importantly, he highlighted two words: conviction and confidence.

God created you for advancement and not so much for failure. Certainly, he believes that you should accomplish the things you require and that you should prosper.

Therefore, equip yourself with exceptional positive certifications. Increase your self-assurance, and it will deflect all of your questions. Utilize solid confidence to flourish and achieve abundance in all aspects of your life.

Chapter 12: The Dexterous Art Of Negotiation

The essence of leadership is communication. Occasionally, this involves informing someone of news. Occasionally, this requires advocating for your skills, and occasionally, it requires attempting to find common ground and reach an agreement. The process of reaching a compromise with someone who wants different things is the essence of negotiating, and it is one of the most crucial leadership skills you must develop. There is negotiation at all levels and within all business relationships. You may negotiate prices for services with clients, or you may negotiate your salary with your employer. Every circumstance in which opposing parties must reach an agreement requires negotiation. This chapter examines the various components of negotiation and teaches you how to add exceptional negotiating skills to your leadership toolkit.

What Is Bargaining?

We've already defined negotiation as a process of compromise, but how exactly does it work? Typically, both parties will present their arguments. Basically consider this situation as an illustration: Your client requests a refund because they believe they received subpar services. You believe that your employees performed admirably and have already been compensated, so the refund would have to come out of the company's budget. The opposing view is straightforward: Your client requests a full refund, but you believe the circumstances do not warrant one. You may believe you are in the right, but so does the client; therefore, you will have to find a way to agree.

The client may acknowledge that the work was good, but not what was expected, and you agree that the client should receive what they desire.

Eventually, you arrive at a solution that falls somewhere in the middle, such as repeating the work at a reduced cost or adapting it substantially. This type of situation will recur frequently in the business world, and the ability to reach a compromise in such disagreements is crucial.

However, negotiations are not always reactive. In employer-employee and client-contractor relationships, negotiation is also a component of establishing a business relationship. Every business relationship requires the formation of an agreement, typically in the form of a contract. You must negotiate the terms of your business relationship prior to the emergence of any disputes. This usually involves monetary compensation, but it can also include hours, vacation time, health insurance, retirement benefits, and anything else related to your job or benefits. Typically, employees and contractors wish to earn as much as possible, whereas employers and clients wish to pay as little as possible. This is not always the case, but it is the foundation of the push-pull relationship between those receiving payment and those making payments. As an employee, you will sell your skills in the hopes of receiving a higher salary, whereas as an employer, you may emphasise the quality of the work environment over salary. Before entering into any professional relationship, it is essential to negotiate so that all parties are satisfied from the outset. There is always room for renegotiation, but everything begins with the initial contract. As a leader, you may be required to negotiate with superiors, clients, and employees, making your negotiation skills a trifecta of distinct abilities.

Teammates can also engage in negotiations. These negotiations tend to focus more on tasks than on money, ensuring that each team member cooperates appropriately and assumes an equal amount of responsibility. There will be some discussion regarding diverse skill sets and work ethics during negotiations regarding the distribution of work and responsibilities. They may occur among employees, or you may be required to mediate the negotiation. As a leader, you must therefore possess exceptional negotiating skills. You will need to personally negotiate and mediate discussions. In the mediation phase, you will need to be objective so that your employees can see both sides of the argument and reach a compromise that feels fair to both parties. This competency will help you just lead your team to new heights of collaboration and productivity.

How to Bargain

But how does one negotiate? What are the essential elements of a successful negotiation? The process of negotiation can appear complicated. You may be concerned about overplaying your hand if you do not always get exactly what you desire. This is the general path you must just take during negotiations. Even though you really want to obtain the best possible deal, you risk offending or repelling your client if you are too aggressive or rigid.

Conversely, you run the risk of appearing too timid and leaving the negotiation having conceded more than you desired. Basically consider negotiation in terms of marketplace bartering. As a shopkeeper, you really want to charge the highest possible price while preventing the customer from leaving. It is a delicate art that must be practised accordingly. A skilled negotiator is able to play with a firm but flexible hand, making their desires clear while remaining receptive to the other side's proposals. There are four primary phases to the negotiation procedure. In this section, we will dissect these four crucial facets of negotiation so that you can become a savvy marketer who refuses to accept no for an answer.

Developing Your Position

Before entering into any negotiation, you must ensure that you have a thorough understanding of the terms. Learn every aspect of the required work and have your overhead and profit margins readily available. You should also be acutely aware of market averages, ensuring that you are not grossly exceeding or falling below the norm. If you have all of these numbers in front of you, you can negotiate terms more intelligently. You can ensure that neither your margins nor the prices of your services fall below the market rate. Providing precise information will simple make it easier to persuade a client. Saying something along the lines of, "The going rate for this type of service is X, we are willing to offer you Y," or "This service costs us X to produce, so I can charge you no less than Y." If you are prepared and familiar with all the numbers, you will appear knowledgeable and reasonable and will be able to simple make decisions immediately.

Emotional Self-Preparation

The other aspect of preparation for negotiations is emotional. Depending on the stakes of your negotiation, you may be under considerable stress. However, it is best to negotiate with a clear head and a calm demeanour. You do not really want to become angry or anxious during the negotiation and lose control. Before entering the negotiation room, you should ensure that you have dealt with all your emotions. Write a journal entry or have a conversation with a friend about your anxieties. You can even conduct a simulated negotiation in which a trusted individual asks you questions while you practise your responses. These exercises will help you alleviate some of your anxiety and emotionally prepare you for the actual event. You need not just feel weak to perform any of these actions.

Due to this, many lawyers and politicians engage in mock debates before appearing in court or on television. Once you enter the negotiation room, you will have gotten rid of all your anxiety and be fully prepared for any curveballs your opponents may throw at you. Therefore, in addition to being factually prepared for your negotiation, you should also be emotionally prepared for the stress that the process can bring. If you ensure adequate preparation on both fronts, you will dominate the negotiation!

Chapter 13: Universal Obstacles

You will invariably encounter certain universal roadblocks as you navigate in the direction you have chosen for yourself. You are likely aware of the dangers of associating with negativity, but there are other attitudes that can send you on a long detour. Among the most significant are guilt, inferiority/superiority, seriousness, self-sacrifice, and the inability to receive. You would be surprised at how frequently these thoughts hijack your attention, particularly when they attach to your conditioning and create a story you believe. These attitudes are ingrained in human nature, and it requires awareness to recognise them and choose otherwise. Let's examine how Jackie's conditioning was triggered by her inferiority and how she overcame it.

When I first began working with Jackie, she had a profound sense of inferiority and inadequacy. Her mother passed away when she was young, and she felt at least partially responsible. There was no logical explanation for this emotion. As a young child, she emotionally reacted and repeatedly told herself, "If only I were better, my mother wouldn't have left me." She overcompensated for this feeling of deficiency by working excessively hard, which was exhausting her. As a Generator, she has a steady supply of energy, but she struggles to say no to requests. This issue can be exacerbated by The Gate of Power, Gate 34 (see Graph C), leading to burnout. I worked with her to uncover and release her childhood self-defeating belief, "I'm not good enough." She was able to cease self-blame. However, years of carrying this programme in her subconscious left her with a lingering inferiority complex. So long as she allowed this feeling to gain a foothold, she would never achieve her objectives.

Inferiority is a universal obstacle that includes superiority as the opposite side of the same coin. Both routes will require a detour. It is natural to desire significance, as this is one of the mind's fundamental needs. The issue is how you deal with the situation. We are programmed by the media to believe in the ideal body type, attitude, lifestyle, and relationships. Obviously, you fall short in comparison; everybody does. When you attempt to fit an ideal or image into your mind, you abandon yourself and the many gifts you possess naturally. Your heart will never support a goal that requires you to be someone you are not. While you stand in front of the mirror requesting significance, the mirror intensifies your desire for more significance.

When Jackie stopped comparing herself to others and began adhering to specific protocols, she was able to overcome her inferiority complex. The world mirror reflected back to her that everything was in order, which bolstered her sense of completeness. People began to respect her more and solicit her opinion on a variety of issues. Her ability to successfully engage at work improved significantly.

Guilt is perhaps the greatest obstacle, as it is deeply ingrained in our current culture and affects nearly everyone. Since early childhood, teachers, religious authorities, and parents have used guilt to manipulate our behaviour. It is accompanied by the notion, "If you're guilty, you must do as I say." To comprehend how dangerous it is to align with this energy, stand in front of a mirror. Put on your best guilty expression and view the image with detachment. How would you describe this individual? The first thing that comes to mind is that they committed an error. Then, my mind begins to basically consider what they could have done, and it usually comes up with something. Continue to observe this guilty face in the mirror. What else can you observe? They are requesting punishment. A signal is being broadcast to anyone who wishes to pick it up: "Please punish me." The mirror will grant your request, and someone will appear in your life to fulfil it. At that point, you may transition into a victim mentality. Why does this keep happening to me? There is no sense of accountability because there is a delay between feeling guilty and receiving punishment. The victim has ample proof that someone else is to blame. While I do not condone the behaviour of the aggressor, your guilty conscience is the true cause of this punishment.

When Sandra contacted me, she recounted a string of misfortunes that had befallen her in recent months. Three months ago, her older sister Vanessa had visited, and they had reminisced about the good old days. Their parents were strict as children, particularly with her older sister. If any of the younger children misbehaved, she was punished. When Sandra made a mistake, her sister would punish her so severely and swiftly that she became traumatised. Sandra's 1/3 learning Profile requires her to simple make errors, as she learns through trial and error. As a result of the swiftness with which she was reprimanded for her errors, she was convinced that something was gravely wrong with her. She walked around with the sense that she was an error. She had learned to let go of this feeling over the years, but her sister's visit reopened old wounds. She relapsed into the habit of feeling guilt, which resulted in a series of unfortunate occurrences, including the theft of her wallet.

As long as she continues to just take the stance that "I've done something wrong so I must be punished," she will continue to invite attacks. Your heart and soul never align with punishment, so this experience is clearly coming from conditioning or old beliefs.

There are many forms of guilt and as Sandra worked through various processes, she was able to reclaim her sense of wholeness. In some cases, it was enough to stop justifying her actions. In other situations, she needed to simple make amends and do some forgiveness work. Eventually she started feeling that all was right with the world. The mirror reflected this back to her. The unfortunate accidents stopped, and she was once again leading her life.

Guilt is insidious. Recently I was working with some community members on this issue. Since it was forefront in my mind, I started noticing places where I still hold guilt on a subtle level. For example, I messaged a client that I would be ten minutes late for our call and asked if that was okay. She agreed. When I got on the call, I started to go into the story of why I needed an extra ten minutes. I caught myself experiencing guilt and stopped talking for a moment. I realised my attention was on myself. I tuned into my client and thought about what she might really want to hear from me. Instead of explaining myself I told her how grateful

I was for those extra ten minutes and thanked her. She didn't really want to hear my stories, and she happily received the compliment.

Guilt keeps you focused on yourself rather than the other person. It crops up in the most unexpected times. Stay aware and awake.

Before we easy move on, let's look briefly at a couple of other common roadblocks – seriousness and self-sacrifice. Where there is seriousness, there is judgement or fear, and the mind has taken hold of you. About twenty-five years ago, my husband and I trekked to the Mount Everest basecamp with a group from REI. Along the way we visited a high Lama in a remote Himalayan village. He blessed us on our journey and tied red prayer strings around each of us. When I remember our visit, I remember his laughter. Even when he wasn't laughing, he looked like he was ready to do so. It made a deep impact on me. Many years later when spiritual masters visited our centre, they would remind us that seriousness closes down access to our guidance and to higher order processes such as compassion. As the Bible says, "Wear the world as a light garment," and you'll have a better perspective. Life is a game, and it takes focus and commitment to easy move through it consciously, not seriously.

When you just think about self-sacrifice, what could be more serious than that? We've already talked about its effect on you and the ones you're trying to help. There's a particular way this roadblock interferes with your goals. Part of self-sacrifice is not allowing yourself to have what you truly want. I find this programme is running in many of my clients, and you can imagine how it stops you from creating the reality you prefer. As soon as you become aware that it's operating, you can you choose differently. Your soul wants to fulfil your desires, so "not allowing yourself to have" is an idea originating from your conditioning. Tap into the heart and reconnect with the joy of receiving. If it's still an issue, we can work through it.

Chapter 14: Understanding Leadership

In a world where innovation is occurring at an accelerated rate, the leadership skills required have also evolved. To better supervise teams and actually develop as leaders, experts must recognise and adapt their individual leadership styles. A 21st-century leadership structure necessitates the utilisation of individuals from both within and outside a team and organisation in order to effectively confront and overcome organisational obstacles and foster innovation. In this chapter, you will gain a deeper understanding of the dynamic nature of leadership.

1.1 What is a Leader?

Leadership is the process of motivating and directing a group or an individual to complete a task. Leaders motivate followers to just take the necessary actions for success. To actually develop into a great leader, you must acquire the necessary knowledge and skills.

There are leaders in every organisation, including consultants, senior managers, and directors. As a subordinate, you could use your leadership skills to mentor new hires or just lead meetings. Depending on the group and the circumstances, each leader may employ a single leadership style or a combination of several.

However, an individual's leadership capacity is significantly determined by their character qualities. Aspiration, commitment, sincerity, honesty, tenacity, and social competence are characteristics frequently associated with leadership. In the earliest stages of leadership research, such characteristics were believed to define great leaders, and researchers sought to identify the characteristics that supported leaders' efficiency and growth within organisations.

By examining these characteristics, we can gain a better understanding of appropriate leadership philosophies and the relationships between different actions and effective leadership. An examination of great leaders reveals that, while certain characteristics may be shared, many vital traits, abilities, personalities, and styles are unique to each individual. Therefore, every child should recognise their effective individual leadership and value their unique qualities, as demonstrated by their characteristics and skills.

1.2 Management Qualities

The following characteristics must be possessed by every successful leader:

Intelligence

The ability to comprehend facts and their relationships, as well as the capacity to reason, perceive, and think, are all components of intelligence, also known as brain capacity or mental skills. Leaders are more intelligent than nonleaders; intelligence-related characteristics typically help individuals attain positions of leadership influence. According to a study, however, a leader's ability to inspire followers may be diminished if their values diverge significantly from those of their followers. Therefore, effective leaders must be willing to convey complex concepts to their followers in a manner that meets their needs.

Confidence and Willpower

Self-assured leaders are confident in their judgement, ideas, capacity, authority, decision-making, and skills. These leaders are self-aware and confident, but not arrogant or conceited. They have a positive outlook on themselves and can continue with the belief that any obstacle can be overcome, even if they simple make the wrong decision. Self-assurance and self-worth are characteristics of influential leaders. They recognise that their leadership will benefit their organisations and that their influence over others is appropriate and legitimate.

The motivation of a leader to simple make a decision is determination, which includes vigour, initiative, persistence, and tenacity. Determined leaders possess the tenacity required to see a task through to completion and persevere in the face of obstacles.

Character

Integrity is primarily characterised by moral character, which is essentially the daily application of personal principles.

Morality, dependability, and integrity are characteristics of effective leaders. Leaders who demonstrate integrity are rewarded with respect, admiration, and the unwavering support of their followers. Interactions between leaders and followers are founded upon integrity. Suppose, however, that a leader is viewed as dishonest. In that case, they will not have the loyalty of their supporters, and it will be difficult for them to maintain relationships with their superiors and subordinates. Integrity in leadership is both assisting followers and recognising that devotion is a two-way street.

Great leaders uphold the same standards for themselves as they do for their followers; to do otherwise would betray the confidence of their followers. When leaders deceive or lie to their subordinates, they erode their subordinates' trust. Abuse, deceit, and empty promises hinder the leader's effectiveness as well. People lose faith in leaders who act in their own self-interest. Effective communication and the dissemination of useful information are hindered if leaders cannot maintain the confidence of their followers. Leaders who do not accept responsibility for their own decisions and actions are viewed as unreliable or even worse, particularly if they attempt to place the blame for their failures on others. Good leadership ceases to exist when personal integrity is compromised.

1.3 Leadership Skills

Management skills are the abilities and abilities that a leader uses to achieve objectives and goals. These three skill categories—technical, interpersonal or humanistic, and conceptual—form the basis of effective leadership. These skills are quite distinct from the personality traits of leaders. Abilities determine what leaders can accomplish, whereas qualities define who they are.

Technical Knowledge

Technical skills include an understanding of the tasks performed by an organisation, its structure, and its norms; competence in specialised tasks; and knowledge of the procedures, tools, and equipment utilised by organisational units. Several methods, including formal education, on-the-job training, and practise, can be utilised to cultivate technical skills. Technical proficiency is essential for administrators in positions of supervision and middle management, but is significantly less crucial for senior managers and those in top management.

Human or Interpersonal Skills

As opposed to technical skills, which include working with objects, this ability is all about interacting with people. Leaders must comprehend how people behave, how groups operate, and the thoughts, emotions, and motivations of their followers. Using their communication skills, influential leaders can collaborate with colleagues, supervisors, and colleagues as well as clients and partners.

Compassion is an essential component of interpersonal skills. It provides the capacity to understand the intentions, values, and emotions of others. Compassion also requires the social intelligence to know what actions are appropriate in particular situations.

A leader must understand what supporters really want and how they perceive a situation in order to choose a practical and persuasive approach.

Continuous self-observation assists leaders in understanding how their behaviour impacts their followers. These leaders are capable of adapting their actions to the circumstances at hand. Effective verbal communication and eloquence are additional social skills that are beneficial to the leadership process of persuasion.

Interpersonal skills are fundamental to effective leadership. Strong interpersonal skills help groups work together more efficiently, encourage the pursuit of shared goals, and enable leaders to employ effective persuasion and perception management strategies.

Conceptual Capabilities

This involves dealing with ideas and concepts, just as technical and social skills involve dealing with objects and people, respectively. Mental talents encompass a variety of qualities, including judgement, instinct, imagination, and forethought. Several conceptual abilities, including inductive and deductive logic, rational thought, intellectual skills, and idea generation, may be assessed by proficiency examinations.

Leaders comprehend how their organisations function and where they should be headed; they must have strong conceptual skills. Effective strategic planning necessitates that executives simple make predictions for the future based on current trends. This is essential for shaping an organization's future, particularly in economically difficult times. Leaders in public health must be able to manage multiple stakeholders and complex relationships. They must comprehend how various organisational components interact with one another and how changes in one region can affect numerous other regions.

In addition, a leader's portfolio of intuition grows as a result of exposure to specific issues. Influential leaders frequently combine conscious thought with insight based on the situation.

Conceptual abilities are the most crucial set of skills for leaders.

1.4 Leader's Character

A leader's persona is a collection of actions and characteristics that illustrate a consistent behavioural strategy that reacts to individuals, objects, and environmental concepts. Personality and the capacity to comprehend the characteristics of followers influence the leadership effectiveness of a leader. Numerous studies into the many facets of personality have led to the discovery of the "big five" personality traits:

Gregariousness

Cooperativeness

Reliability

Emotional Stability

Generosity

Gregariousness

One's level of involvement and interest in things external to themselves. The characteristics and qualities of this dimension significantly influence a leader's behaviour in group situations.

Depending on their sociability and extroversion, people may vary in their comfort level when conversing and meeting new people. People who enjoy being in charge and exerting influence frequently exhibit high levels of self-control and self-assurance. They are willing to compete for leadership positions and have confidence in themselves. Social interactions may exhaust introverts emotionally or physically, necessitating some time alone for reflection and recharging. Numerous leaders value assertiveness, assertiveness, and other extraverted personality traits.

Cooperativeness

Cooperativeness is the capacity to get along with others, and it is commonly believed to include traits such as courtesy, trust, cooperation, and humour. High performers in this area project an upbeat, friendly, optimistic, caring, and compassionate persona. Essentially, they are regarded as having pleasant personalities. The capacity for agreement of a leader is particularly crucial. In general, a leader who is kind and helpful will be well-liked and qualified to resolve conflicts within the organisation. Being affable could help them gain acceptance and supporters for their cause. People with a high level of agreeableness frequently just feel the need to connect with others and with organisations.

Reliability

It is the extent to which an individual is responsible, possesses moral character, and has a strong drive for success. In contrast to those with low dependability, who are frequently impulsive and easily distracted from the task at hand, those with high ethics can focus on specific objectives and pursue them methodically.

Given the nature of their responsibilities, it is appealing to leaders. Frequently, intense concentration is required to address various emerging public and social challenges.

Emotional Stability

Psychoticism has been used to describe the personality trait of emotional maturity in various classification schemes. This element reveals a person's level of composure, security, and social competence regardless of the wording. Self-discipline, self-assurance, and self-respect are crucial components of this aspect. Leaders with high emotional stability can withstand pressure, accept criticism, and learn from their mistakes, whereas leaders with poor dynamic consistency are frequently tense, impatient, anxious, depressed, or lacking in self-confidence.

Generosity

It refers to an individual's levels of intellectual curiosity, inquisitiveness, open-mindedness, and a focus on learning. Individuals with a high level of openness are frequently inventive, creative, and willing to basically consider novel strategies and ideas. In contrast, less adaptable individuals tend to have more specialised interests and frequently prefer the status quo. Since the public health profession places such a strong emphasis on change over stability, openness is an essential quality.

Chapter 15: Decision Making

From the time you awaken until you fall asleep, you simple make a variety of choices. You may not even consciously basically consider the majority of them. Every day, we simple make decisions regarding what to eat, what to wear, how to get to work, and even when to go to sleep. Some are minor, while others are significant, and while some decisions can be made with little thought, others must be deliberate. The decision-making process requires managers to pay close attention to specifics. It is the ability to simple make decisions that yield the best outcomes for your organisation without sacrificing work quality or time management. Interestingly, decision-making is not an innate ability. Rather, it is one that we acquire through past experiences and situations. The good news is that any manager or aspiring manager can do a great deal to enhance his or her ability to simple make prudent and judicious decisions for enhanced productivity and performance.

There are times when the necessity of making a choice can just feel dreadful. During the decision-making procedure, there may be much at stake. It automatically places you in a position of leadership where you must be responsible. There will also be times when you lack the necessary time to carefully basically consider the situation or examine the facts prior to making a decision. Similarly, there will be times when the information immediately accessible to you will not simple make decision-making simple. Worrying about whether you are making the right choice can increase self-doubt and disrupt your work flow or ability to complete tasks. Nevertheless, as the decision-maker, you have options that can just lead to success or failure. Consequentially, it's crucial to train yourself to become an effective decision-maker, as making a poor choice is always a possibility. You can become a better decision-maker by adhering to the framework presented in this chapter.

Identify

The first step in decision-making is determining where the decision really need to be made. This provides a clearer picture of the issue you are actively attempting to resolve. If you do not know what you are dealing with or the nature of the situation, you must just take the time to investigate. You cannot simple make a good decision if you are unfamiliar with the given area or circumstance. Therefore, simple make it a habit to identify the context in which you are required to simple make decisions, whether it pertains to managing client deliverables, time management, or any other workplace activity.

Review

Once you have determined where to focus your attention and what decision must be made, it is time to generate ideas. You cannot simple make an informed decision without taking into account all relevant and accessible information. There will be a great deal of information and data to examine, which can be difficult to navigate and evaluate. Using simple strategies such as mind mapping, flowcharting, or even coloured post-it notes is the most effective way to stay on top of things and remain organised. Depending on the type of learner you are (visual, reader, writer, hands-on, etc.), it is essential that you find a system that allows you to maximise your decision-making efficiency. It will ensure that you do not lose track of crucial information and documents.

Alternatives

Basically consider some potential solutions and outcomes of a specific decision while making a choice. After carefully reviewing the information, you will typically have multiple options. Now is not the time to be concerned about which option is the best. Instead, you must ask questions and pay attention to the responses you receive. As there will likely be a great deal to consider, simple discuss these options with your team members or other trusted individuals within the organisation. In addition, the alternatives you basically consider must align with your organization's methods and objectives.

Evidence

Once you are aware of all possible solutions and outcomes, evaluate their advantages and disadvantages. There's a good chance that even your competitors have dealt with similar decisions in the past. Basically consider their outcomes and the decisions they made, for example in relation to a marketing strategy, an expansion plan, or online visibility. After this, carefully examine the potential gains and losses associated with each of the available options. Basically consider how the specific decision will impact your team members and any other relevant parties. If the decision is tied to a change, basically consider what you must do to adapt and how they will do it. At this stage, you shouldn't rush. The choice you simple make must inspire self-assurance. While it is natural to have doubts, you should not allow them to paralyse your mind to the point where you are unable to concentrate or realistically anticipate the results of your decision. You must be satisfied with the decisions you have made based on the preceding steps.

Choice

You have reached the point where a final choice must be made. After weighing the evidence and reviewing the information as well as the alternatives, it is time to simple make a decision and just take a stand. Learn to rely on yourself when performing this task. Have faith in your abilities and trust your instincts. Remember that you have the necessary qualifications to simple make this call. It is common knowledge that making a decision can be frustratingly stressful. Depending on a number of factors, including your work style, ethics, personality, and the entrusted responsibilities, you may be second-guessing yourself. That is typical. However, as a responsible and organised manager, you must have confidence in your ability to formulate a decision that will benefit the organisation as a whole. As we've seen, there is no such thing as a "perfect" decision. Therefore, rely on your judgement and don't attempt to simple make a "perfect" decision.

Act

A decision devoid of action is absurd. Now is the time to execute the decision. Focus on developing a strategy that will bring your team and organisation closer to its objectives. Strategic planning can be time-consuming, but it is essential to a successful outcome. Also, execution is crucial because even the best plan can fail if it is poorly carried out. While the specifics are entirely up to you, it is essential that you include all interested parties in your action plan so that everyone knows what to expect as a result of your managerial decision.

Reflect

Reflection is the final step of the decision-making process. It is not simply a matter of deciding and proceeding to the next ones. Instead of rushing through the process, just take some time to review and reflect. You may also determine a better course of action for future decisions or address issues that impeded the final results and outcomes. Basically consider all of the applicable skills and what you would do differently next time. This step is not intended to determine whether you made the correct decision. Instead, it is about considering honestly whether you have done your best, as well as what worked and what did not.

Consider, for instance, whether the identified problem was resolved. How efficient was the process of gathering information? Were your established objectives met? If you made mistakes at any point, record them. As a manager, you have a good chance of enhancing your decision-making abilities if you learn from every decision you make.

Obstacles to Overcome

When it comes to effective decision-making, most managers face the following obstacles:

Too much information or too little knowledge can be extremely confusing. You can only effectively prioritise and select essential information through practise. In turn, this facilitates decision-making. If necessary, conduct additional research prior to deciding.

It is essential to have confidence in the decisions you make. However, excessive confidence can be detrimental. In spite of your best efforts, there will be times when you simple make the incorrect choice. This is a normal part of life. Therefore, remember to acknowledge the possibility of making mistakes.

3. Correctly identifying a problem or situation in which a decision must be made is an crucial aspect of the decision-making process. You cannot expect the final decision to yield the desired results if you incorrectly identify the target.

The final obstacle you must overcome is ensuring that everyone is on board with your decision. You are the team's final decision-maker. Collaboration is impossible, however, unless the entire team is kept informed. In this process, you will need to be transparent and ensure that your team is aware of the decision-making process and criteria.

As a manager, you are tasked with making decisions every day. Once you have learned to recognise, evaluate, and implement your decisions, it will be easier for you to simple make decisions that everyone can support when necessary. Remember that honesty and transparency are essential components of this, and that you cannot promote a healthy collaborative framework without involving others and explaining your method. You owe your collaborators a certain level of transparency, which, when met, inspires their trust and encourages them to accept your decision.

Chapter 16: How To Become An Effective Leader

Certain prerequisites must be met before a person can be considered a competent leader. They consist of:

Set The Right Example To Become A Leader:

It is essential for leaders to set the proper example and serve as role models for how they really want their followers to behave and perform. As you establish the staff's expectations, all eyes are on you and following your every move. If your leadership team is well-groomed and punctual in the mornings, this will inspire your employees to follow suit. They will evaluate your willingness to roll up your sleeves and dig in to achieve your team's goals, your ability to communicate at all hierarchical levels, and your level of accountability when things go wrong. If you really want your staff members to be as professional as you are, it is essential that you serve as a positive example.

In everything you do at work, set an exemplary standard. If you are a habitual offender, it might be challenging to criticise a staff member for anything.

Continuous Development Of Your Leadership Abilities:

To become a great leader, you must acknowledge your abilities and limitations. Seeking continuous self-improvement entails the development of one's own skill set and the assurance that one possesses the necessary leadership skills.

Learn why it is so crucial to engage in self-reflection.

Be technically proficient:

To be a successful leader, you must also be one step ahead of your team when it comes to disruptive technologies in your industry. By subscribing to industry blogs and reading whitepapers, you can stay abreast of technological advancements in your field. No one is claiming that you must be an expert in everything, but you should understand the challenges and opportunities presented by technological advancements to your organisation.

4. Simple make Reasonable And Timely Decisions:

You must be able to simple make informed decisions immediately. You will be in a strong position to just lead your team if you are well-versed in effective problem-solving, decision-making, and planning techniques.

5. Accept And Seek Accountability For Your Actions:

As a leader, your team will look to you for guidance, inspiration, and strategies to propel the company to new heights. People will look to you to just take corrective and decisive action when things go awry. Your response to adversity affords you the opportunity to set an example of a strong leader.

6. Positive Attitude:

A favourable work environment is more likely to foster an engaged and productive workforce. By displaying enthusiasm and self-assurance, a competent leader will recognise their potential influence in this work environment.

It is not always possible for a leader to have a positive outlook on every task they will undertake, but the more negativity you can prevent from harming your team, the more likely you are to see positive results.

Keep your coworkers informed:

Your employees will expect you to be up-to-date at all times, so strive to remain abreast of all developments in your company and industry.

You will then be able to impart this information to your team, who will hopefully value your efforts.

Effective communication is essential to becoming a successful leader.

Learn About Your Team:

David Brent, the affable CEO from the BBC's The Office, wanted to be friends with everyone. His managerial strategy was to be entertaining, or, if you prefer, the office clown. Unfortunately, people quickly lost respect for him due to this management style, and he was incapable of managing himself, let alone a team.

Management requires you to maintain a certain degree of separation from your staff. You should always keep in mind that your team will be comprised of individuals with diverse perspectives, skills, and stages of their careers. Therefore, it is essential to comprehend what motivates people and to keep in mind that what motivates one person may not necessarily motivate another.

Do Not Be Afraid To Delegate:

One of the most crucial things a team leader must understand immediately is the importance of delegation. Successful delegation begins with the proper assignment of individuals to tasks. If there are gaps in the skill sets of team members, a skilled leader will be able to immediately detect and address these gaps.

Ensure Duties Are Comprehended, Supervised, And Completed:

Before assigning a task to a member of your team, you must understand what is required and what an acceptable outcome would look like.

If your team asks you questions about the assignment, you should be prepared with responses. Some team members may lose respect for you if you do not have the necessary knowledge on hand.

Chapter 17: You Need To Remain Humble

Thank you for listening, everyone. Then, we will proceed to the seventh key. I would like to pull over, stop, and park here, however. In response to a specific question, have you identified any new methods and opportunities for personal development thus far? Until now, you have utilised a variety of keys.

I am unaware of your progress on each key. If you've obtained it. You have identified new methods and opportunities for personal development. I need your response and feedback so I can better prepare for this peer recovery support and leadership training today, as well as for any future books I may write.

Have you identified new methods and opportunities for personal growth, not just for your organisation or for your recovery period or participants, or whatever you may have referred to them as at your organisation? However, in general, have you identified any new methods and opportunities for personal development? Okay, welcome to the seventh key, number seven.

I am known as Sobia. I established the Minor Adjustments Program. We appreciate your participation in this recovery. Support and leadership development This is the seventh key. Very significant. You must stay humble. The first bullet point on the screen reads, "First, determine what you're building, what you're building, your foundation." Similarly, when working with a recovery participant or client, you must first determine what you're building, their foundation.

Remember that the deeper the foundation is dug or the deeper they build before building upward, the taller the building will be. Therefore, the majority of the time, a large number of people have diverse foundations. We are addressing multiple avenues to recovery. If there are multiple routes to recovery and we have established a foundation in our lives, we must comprehend. Find out what you're building your foundation for first, and then you can better assist the people you're dealing with, because not everyone who comes to us will agree with our foundation.

This does not imply that we are qualified or able to assist these individuals. However, we must have a concrete understanding of our foundation. If we understand our foundation, we will be better equipped to assist the individuals who seek our services. Why is this significant, and why am I bringing it up? I'll give you an example. My spiritual foundation serves as the basis for the development of my character and integrity. What does that imply?

This means that I will interact with the individuals I am interacting with and ensure that my behaviour is ethically sound because I have character and integrity. Therefore, I will not do anything to them regardless of how they may behave. I will not treat them differently than the standard that I have established for myself. That is my starting point. Find out what you're basing your foundation on, and you will be in a better position to assist these individuals.

Remember, first determine what you build in your foundation, and then you'll be in a better position to assist the individual in the following bullet point. You must learn to be confident and humble. And this is so beneficial for me. You must learn to be confident and humble. And don't let your humility diminish your confidence.

Many people believe that a person cannot simultaneously be confident and humble. False, you may do so. You can be both modest and assured. I am modest enough. Let me explain to you. I am sufficiently humble to recognise that I received the gifts and abilities necessary to accomplish my vocation. However, I am self-assured enough to know that no one can maximise my talent. Then, I. You can see the distinction. You must be both humble and confident. You must be humble enough to recognise that you received your strategy, your talents, your gift, and everything else you possess.

However, you must be self-assured enough to recognise that nobody can maximise what you have like you. When you are both confident and humble, or humble and confident, you can allow your humility to diminish your confidence. You must memorise these two items.

Not to worry about those who misunderstand your confidence. This demonstrates arrogance. Some people recognise you as the counsellor that you are, and you do so with self-assurance. You are confident as a director of the organisation, as well as a supervisor, and as a peer recovery support specialist.

However, you must learn how to be both humble and confident, and you must not allow your humility to diminish your confidence.

Concern yourself not with those who misjust take your confidence for arrogance. Listen to me. You can be confident in your position while remaining humble enough to recognise that it was bestowed upon you by something greater than yourself. You can be modest in this regard, but you must have confidence in who you are. Nobody can extract more from you than you can from yourself, period.

In any domain or arena. You must stay humble, I get it. However, you must learn to be both modest and confident. Next, you must learn to be confident and humble. And you do not allow your modesty to diminish your self-assurance. Concern yourself not with those who misjust take your confidence for arrogance. The third bullet is the next to be stated. Always preceding promotion is humility. This implies that humility will always precede promotion. You must be humble. Having humility is an admirable trait. This is something you possess. Before being promoted, you must improve in this area. In this peer support for recovery leadership training. Seventhly, you must maintain your humility. Why is this important, and why am I even bringing it up in this particular training? Because I know that if you follow the advice I am giving you, you will receive a promotion because you will begin to actually develop in an area of your expertise that other people have not yet accomplished.

And they wish to know where you obtained this strategy. And you can tell them always Mike Where provided me with leadership training and peer recovery support through the Minor Adjustments Program. If you follow these keys, I will reveal a tried-and-true strategy that I have employed for the past 14 years, and I have been promoted at every step of my career. However, humility always precedes my promotion, which means it precedes it.

You must maintain humility, but you must remember. Do not allow your humility to diminish your confidence. You must maintain your humility no matter what. I can almost guarantee that you will receive promotions if you implement the strategies I'm sharing today.

The following item is titled The Wardrobe of humility. I have these as a result of kidnapping Gloria Copeland. I came across it all while reading it one day, and as someone who likes to teach others about humility, I knew that if you follow the strategies I employ, you will begin to see advancement in any area of your life.

If you employ the same strategies I have employed. And I've observed that humility is one of the traits that we must cultivate, because if you lack humility, your promotion will eventually resemble this bandage. And Mr. and Mrs. Gloria Copeland had written something that was effective. It states that they will coach. They referred to it as the wardrobe of modesty. Now, observe this. It says, Humility. Basically consider this first. Now, what I really want you to do as a professional is to put yourself ahead of any degrees you may or may not possess. I really want you to basically consider me when I read and basically consider you. Who among the individuals with whom we are dealing puts others first? That is exactly the type of person we are.

We advocate for individuals who suffer from substance use disorders. So he considers others. Indigenous groups advocate for others. Humility places others before oneself. Now, let's see. The second definition of humility is contentment behind the scenes. You know, we can have a spotlight recovery where we put the person we help in the spotlight and they give us permission to put them on a pedestal and tell everyone how well they have been doing in their recovery walks. And we can be in the background.

Yes, humility is content in the background. We can showcase our recoveries, our participants, and our clients, and we intend to let people know this. However, you used to speak negatively about this person or their life, but this person's life has since improved. We are able or humbly able to remain in the background; put them in the spotlight, and we will cheer for them.

You can see how this applies to our lives and professions. This is the attire of modesty. Humility considers ourselves first. This indicates that they advocate for individuals. Two, she is content behind the scenes, which means we can give our recovery participants and clients some applause and high-fives. And behind the scenes, we would affirm, "Yes, girl, you've got it."

Yes, you've got it, young man. Third, it states that humility does not force its way to the front. Remember that I stated that humility always precedes a promotion. Therefore, you will not have to push your way to the front. Listen to me. If you maintain humility, the positions you are destined to obtain will propel you to the forefront. There is no need to fight for it.

You are not required to advance to the front. Humility does not exert himself to the forefront. Next, no, because you voluntarily submit. There may be aspects of your organisation that you dislike. I understand that you may not agree with them. You may believe that you should not be treated that way. And I get it. However, you will be submissive to the authority figure who has placed you in a more advantageous position within your organisation than anyone else.

I assure you that if you voluntarily submit to authority, you do not have to agree with every decision that is made; it is acceptable for your agency to simple make decisions that you do not agree with. But if you are willing to submit to those in authority over you, it improves your chances of being promoted. This is evidence of the peer recovery support leadership strategy you can employ, which is disliked by the majority of people.

I have been using this method for the past 14 years, and it has never failed me. Number five, he merely accepts graciously. What is this phrase? Large term, corrections Humility accepts correction with grace. This means that when we are wrong, we are able to see corrections; in this particular key, key number seven, it is acceptable to remain modest. You must accept corrections graciously. I know you believe you are always correct. No, you don't. It's OK. However, humility accepts correction graciously.

I keep saying and I keep emphasising it. I am aware that we are dealing with a group of professionals. Nonetheless, humility, the reception. Correct. If money does not ruin an apology with an excuse, number six. Excuses do not trump an apology in terms of humility. I have been around people in increasingly senior positions, such as supervisors and directors, who say something and then realise they should not have said it because it may have misdirected the individual.

So now they return and attempt to cover it up, ruining the apology with an explanation. Well, I said it because of this, and a lack of humility does not destroy an apology with an excuse. If you must apologise to someone, apologise immediately. We do not require an explanation or justification for your actions. If you work your way to recovery, a client participates, or whatever you may refer to them as, and you simple make a misjust take somewhere.

It is acceptable to apologise to them. Simply avoid giving them an excuse. seventh chapter, modesty Accept accountability. And does this reading shift responsibility? Accepting responsibility does not absolve him of blame. Simply accept responsibility, regardless of how it may appear from a professional standpoint. Avoid shifting the blame. There have been numerous instances in which I have been blamed for things I did not do.

And I assert that I did not do so. I was unaware of that. He accepts responsibility without shifting the blame. However, if something occurs and the individual refuses to accept responsibility, do not panic. Eventually, they must accept responsibility and avoid shifting blame. And finally, number eight, your favourite word will be humility; humility will adapt. Again, this is the seventh key.

You must stay humble. This is peer support for recovery and leadership development. Of the Minor Adjustments Program, Sobia. The first of the seven keys is to maintain your humility. Determine the basis upon which you are building your structure. You must learn to be confident and humble. And don't let your humility diminish your confidence. And do not worry about these individuals.

Who misinterprets your self-assurance for arrogance. Always preceding your promotion is your humility. Finally, the attire of humility. Humility considers this. First, modesty is contentment. Behind the curtain. Humility does not vie for the forefront. Humility, voluntarily submitting humility, gracefully receiving correction's humility Do not ruin an apology with an explanation.

www.ingramcontent.com/pod-product-compliance
Lightning Source LLC
Chambersburg PA
CBHW050254120526
44590CB00016B/2347